I0437312

From the Psychoanalysis Mind Black
Of an Intelligent ^ man from the Project

By

John Edward F.

Order this book online at www.trafford.com
or email orders@trafford.com

Most Trafford titles are also available at major online book retailers.

Printed in Victoria, BC, Canada.

ISBN: 978-1-4269-3273-1 (sc)

ISBN: 978-1-4269-3274-8 (e-book)

*Our mission is to efficiently provide the world's finest, most comprehensive
book publishing service, enabling every author to experience success.
To find out how to publish your book, your way, and have it available
worldwide, visit us online at www.trafford.com*

Trafford rev. 5/28/2010

 www.trafford.com

North America & international
toll-free: 1 888 232 4444 (USA & Canada)
phone: 250 383 6864 ♦ fax: 812 355 4082

Contents

Digging for Black Gold 'To Drill or not to be Drilled, Is the Future that we must face' 81

Biography

Born in Rockville Centre, Long Island-New York; yet spend most of my youth in Far Rockaway, Queens-New York, seeing the trapped dark cloud hovering over, growing up in a disturb neighborhood of drugs, guns, and gangs. By overcoming and surfacing from the negative of what society thinks of young Black men. Being raised with a strong and tough loving parent has shown my little brother and I the true respect for us and the betterment of future generations to come.

Attended Liberty University in Lynchburg, Virginia for two years, where he then transfers to University of Delaware becoming President of the Martin Luther King Jr.'s Humanities Community Housing. A graduated of the ITT Technical Institute with an Associate of Applied Science in Computer Network System with an emphasis on IT Project Management. An active member of the Gamma Beta Phi Honors Society; elected as a Hero Leader for the 1199 – S.E.I.U Union and volunteered as a Campaign Organizer for the presidential & mayoral election; also a formal member of the NAACP.

This book tells short but realistic details of what I believe minorities' art to do to challenge themselves in order to revolutionize for the better and the perceptive of oneself, through the various topics/issues that is written.

My First Written Book

...From Grade School

By

John E. Farmer

'A day of remembrance can lead to a life time of memories'

Awaken by the powerful sun's ray with it warmest and clear light shinning upon my face, combine with the cool breeze as it enters through the window. As the winds travels through the window guards across the room of a six story building; the little ones, chirping out for more food. I rise up to look out; I can hear the seagulls prying over the ocean as the wave crash gently against the rock. I take a deep breath…Ahhh, three blocks away, and I can still smell the salt from the ocean. I get up, slide into my bedroom shoes (which most called it slippers), and make up my bed, and then I walk over to the door, looking out down the hall from my room. There I can hear my mother, frying the thick slab of bacons, as the fats give off a popping sizzling sound. So, I headed toward the kitchen for my mom and as I enter, there I heard a deep voice from across the table, "good morning!" with the excitement in his voice. "There's my first born son", as he rose from the chair and walk toward me. There he stands looking down at me, standing strong and bold with hands at least two feet in length. He has to be at least nine maybe ten feet tall. I am afraid of him, even thro he love me dearly, because I am his first child. He bends down from the waist and lifted me up with a toss toward the ceiling. As I looked down toward his dark brown shinning face with eyes dark surrounded by a ring of milky white as they are being seen from a far. As I came falling back down toward the ground, he catches me underneath my arm at his knee level. A catch with a stop, except everything within me felt like a ghost fell out of my body.

Therefore, as we leave the apartment, there it hangs waiting for us to aboard. We got on, I watch the first door shut, and there my father pressed the letter 'L'. The second door roll shut and we are hauled down in a smooth and quiet motion. I watched as the light assail from the small rectangle glass, as we pass each level. Passing five levels, the iron box gave a quick bounce, a ding and then the door rolls open.

As we step out of the building, there the first thing that hit me was the warmness from the sun. I feel revitalize, happy, smiling…free, like it was heaven. I'm three and I'm heading off for Head Start.

'For many, many years as men grow; men learn to develop knowledge to which they tend to shape and mode themselves throughout their lives to become old and wise'.

I can recall many days of achieving many new words and moving onto the next grade level. I remember back in Daycare of the year 1975, where everyone sat facing the Caretakers with amazement to my eyes as I watched the aluminum Jiffy pan being shaken back and forth, side to side as the Caretaker kept the flames from the big iron low. That wonderful aroma put the hunger in us, as we slip the heavy concentrated, no sugar orange juice, the one that is made from the frozen can.

Then I hear her voice saying, "O.K., it's about to being." with excitement in her voice. Everyone cram closer, but not too close to the big iron, and then within second; "pop"…"pop"…"pop, pop"…"pop-pop"…"pop, pop, pop, pop"…"pop, pop, pop, pop, pop". As the Jiffy pan expanded, busting open, and overflowing with the golden popcorn.

After the popping has ended, the Caretakers quickly checked to see if all of us were o.k. As we all lay still on the floor, seeing two bullets hole through the window. I lifted my head up toward the big iron for the aluminum Jiffy pan, in which it was lying on the floor. Seeing the tears dropping from one of the Caretakers' eyes, I glance toward the front of the big iron to see what the Caretaker was looking at, and there…one, just one beautiful popcorn laying there while the rest of the seeds in the pan was burnt. No other kids was able to understand what had happen to the rest of the popcorns or why they didn't pop out, however, there was one young boy who knew why and that when I quickly develop the knowledge.

Whenever I leave that day-care center, I know that one day I will return, to give hope to those that will be here after me. To let them know that this world can be a wonderful place; if we can work together. However, what choice do I have, what I want to be when I grow-up? What will I become?

I'm now three and a half years old and it another year. I hop into the back seat of the brown Pontiac Firebird. As I always wonder where we were going, mother would say 'We're going bye-bye'; which either means that we are going shopping or visit a relative.

"Daddy!"… "Yes, John" (with a calm voice)…"my finger!" – "Got dammit!" as he roll down the window. "Sit back in the seat! What you doing with your finger out the window for! I told you before, when you get in the car; you sit back in the seat. You can still see out of the window! And don't, do it again! – You hear me!" – I begin to cry, not because of my father yelling at me, but because I made a mistake; well I was pretty much a busy-bee.

'A love story is not just about love, but the caring of one's affection'

I can recall when living out in Springfield Garden, New York. In which my father repeatedly tell the story to the whole world about me leaving the house to play in the front yard. It all begins in the bedroom on the second floor playing with my toys & my father in his room on the bed watching an old western film (John Wade) on Television. So my father suggests that he should take a little rest, because he had worked the night shift. Therefore, my father got up, went downstairs to lock the screen door, leaving the other door open, so that the cool breeze can come in – right upstairs through the house. As he enter the room, before laying unto the bed, he look down at me, with his hand on his hip, pointing with his right finger, saying to me. "Now I want you and Daisy (the dog) to stay in this room, while I take a short nap. Daisy! I want you to keep an eye on John – o.k. Girl?" 'Woof!' – As Daisy bark.

Therefore, I play with my toys cars (the matchbox kinds), as Daisy lay and watch me, as I crash the toys together. Then I heard my father snore…I get up to check to see if he's really sleep. His eyes are close, so I quietly walk down the stairs. Daisy; who is the same age as I am; jump in front of me and growl, but I continue on; on toward the screen door. I tip toe to unlock the latch. I look back with a head jerk to see if my father is still sleeping. Daisy and I step out – down the four steps onto the front yard, without realizing that when the door shut, it will lock itself and before I could turn back, I hear the click. I turn quickly; trying to open the door…it won't open. Daisy, as she sat in front of me and look with an interesting look, both ears up with her head tilted to the side, like she trying to understand. A look that said, 'Hey, I try to tell you'. Knowing that I had done something wrong, I begin to cry and within second, out comes a shadow, looking down at me saying, "Didn't I told you not to go outside"? I try to cry over his voice as he continues, "this is a lesson for you to learn". Daisy begins to howl in my defense, I hope. "You too, Daisy…you were supposes to watch John and make sure he didn't leave the room". Then we both begin to cry louder at the same time. Then one of the neighbors came over in a joked way and asks my father. "Mr. Farmer! What're you doing to the boy?", "Teaching him a lesson". While my father and the neighbor, talk amongst themselves and about me not listening. Later then my father unlocks the latch and the lock itself; after all, he probably waited until I step out, to lock the screen door. This is one true lesson I honor most and that is to obey your parent.

I found out later in life, as I have gotten older, that my father was never sleep. He was observant at every moment even when he was exhausted. Cause you see, my mother worked in the day, and my father worked at night. He let me play or in other words, he let me tired myself out, knowing that Daisy and I will be taking a catnap, two hours after my mom left for work.

This is one memory that I will eternally remember.

Thanks to my parent.

HOW TO BECOME A CROOK...

I MEAN A C.E.O.

BY

John E. Farmer

Why some Companies need to be investigates?

The reason why I feel that some major as well as minor companies art to be investigated, well the reasons for this are the lacks of information is that are kept secretly from the employees. Such as meeting that are met, which can change the outlooks on how employees responds through their works, the effects can cause the employees to have a change in their attitudes, less output of work loads, and being guarded in their owns surrounding.

Attitude that are being raised within the companies, show the unhappiness of the employees; with more demand of work output suitable, to lesser paid. Many companies tend to reward their employees by giving pizza parties or words of "You did a Great job!" with a pat on the back.

Employees also respond to companies by giving out-less productive work, because of how C.E.O. (Chief Executive Officer) gains more dollars while the workers are receiving less. The companies do not seem to understand that the rate that the C.E.O. paid to their employees can and will stress the level of crimes. Such as robbery, stealing, and may causes death to those who may try to stop the unemployed from eating. Reason for better paid at work is the cause of transportations, such as trains, buses, and cabs or how about the high cost of living expenses, such as rent or mortgage, school and property's taxes. Companies must also bear in mind that employees have to purchase clothing, foods, insurances (if we can afford it, from the choice of Medicare the company carries), and many others. All these expenses go up yearly, except for our paid...well, maybe an abysmal quarter. Wow! That is a big hoist. While our indebtedness' bosses, receives over at least (110%) in raises. I know what you may be saying, where are the facts? Well, my facts comes from the Daily News - Special Report of many executives whose cash bonus was 871.5 times the annual wages of the average New Yorker who works for a living. There was and could be still iconic CEO, Sanford Weill of Citigroup and Primerica, who personifies the modern Citi, and his $46.3 million paycheck, is part of the formula. His base salary was $1 million; his cash bonus was $17 million; his "other annual compensation", of $683,684; restricted stock awards of $8 million; stock granted of $3.6 million; stock options exercised of $16 million. Yet, to be collected is another $40.7 million in unexercised options from past years (Daily News, 09/04/02). In addition, who know how many more he may have hidden. Knowing many of you still remember about Enron. Well, "Citi knew what Enron was doing, assisted in the deception and profited from their actions" (Daily News, 09/04/02).

The company I believe that had gotten away with great profits and hidden taxable wealth was Caldor, Stern's, and First Card. Many employees knew that the big C.E.O.s was getting very, very large checks, while those beneath them were either lay-off or given a selvage package.

Is It Legal In What They Do?

Imagine starting and owning your own business putting in the funds and hard work, so that you can have financial freedom. Someone comes along to seek work, you give that person the job assuming that you are doing a good deed for that person, but you paid that individual a little above the nominal hourly pay, expecting ten times the productivity. Is this fair? Well, it the same for the CEOs. Therefore, each and everyone must understand the positions of the CEOs, as well as, those whose work for the companies.

'Everything that you do is legal, until you are caught'. This is the same way with CEOs. They always have something hidden in their back pockets to keep employees paid as low and as long as they can. They also tried to get as much productivity in little time in order to gain wealth. 'Paid low-sell high' seem to be the way for the success of businesses.

Do They Deserve The Pays They Get?

According to the articles about the CEOs and many others, top Executives, not that they get top salary, but if they worked so hard to make their company so superior, then maybe they do deserve a bonus. However, what about the employees who are making the companies grow; do they deserve a big bonus as well?

Let us focus on the issues of the CEOs. They had to come up with idea of ways to market their products. Using the brainpower of how, when, and where to get their products out to the public. Many meeting that have met almost on a daily basic, having to be able to meet the deadline. Many unlimited hours had put in to better their company.

Everywhere and everything that the CEO's does is strictly about business. Whether they go to lunch, at home or on vacation their works never end. They eat, sleep, and think 24/7 about their work. They are responsible for keeping the business running. Their businesses are theirs livelihoods. The public or I should say, those who never owned a business should imagine getting up four or five in the morning, checking the money section in your local newspaper, heading off to work to get the business in operational status and checking to make sure that everything is up and running.

They Make More $$$ When They Lay Off, Downsize or Merge

About ten years ago, many companies tend to downsize their employees due to the lacks of demand or the selling of the product. In which, the store manager had to lay off employees in order to accumulate their situation. However, the true actuality behind all this is that employees do not have to be lay off, regardless of less work. Because if this was the case, then why the CEOs keep getting more affluent?

Store manager, who tried to find raison d'être to fire employees, would try to put more workload on their shoulder or try to irritate them, hoping that they will relinquish. This is one of the reasons they try to prevaricate the employees from retrieving redundancy. By workers who claim for unemployment can steer money from the company through insurance. Nevertheless, less claim of unemployment saves the company money as well as, increasing capital into their pockets.

During the laying off period, this increase the workloads to the fewer workers that are still at the job, mounting additional presser to look for job elsewhere. Because of the overloads of labor, wherein it does not equivalent to the lack of compensate.

Let take a look at Jamie Dimon who is the Chairman and CEO of Bank One, earned his stripes as Citigroup

Chairman Weill's top lieutenant, who demonstrated his talent by downsizing staff, in which he earned a healthy $4 million salary and bonus (New York Post, Friday, 01/16/04, Erica Copulsky and Jenny Anderson). On the other hand, how about the J.P. Morgan CEO William Harrison, who in fact will walk away with company stock valued at $159 million dollars?

In the article, that was written by Paul Tharp of the New York Post stated that Bill Harrison will get a lifetime pension of about $900,000 plus a separate $2.04 million partnership that the bank set up for Mr. Harrison, well as Mr. Harrison's already collected $20 million in bonuses for handling the merger of J.P. Morgan and Chase.

It is also same in the music industry. An article that was written by Phyllis Furman of the Daily News, wrote why Arista records is making a major change. Arista Records that will boot Antonio (L.A.) Reid; who has acquire La Face Records, the label co-founded by Reid and his partner, songwriter Babyface, because of his (Reid) disastrous highly paid artists like Pink, Toni Braxton, and the new TLC had flopped, losing an estimated $100 million. BMG and Sony Music are looking to merge in order to cut costs (which are the employees) and consolidate its labels (in order to gain more money from you and I) in hope to propel back to the top (01/14/2004, Daily News).

So, don't let no one tell you that the economy is down or had to lay off because of the company budgets…these words that are use is full of BULL…well you know what I about to said.

It is all common sense, when there is less demand or work; there is no need for overtime, as well as shorter hour and less workers.

Learn the Games They Play

In order to understand the business, many must be good listeners. You cannot just be educated in the field, but must know how the field is structure in order to play in it. How long and wide the field is or how many can come unto the field.

This may have happened too many of you who seen jobs or careers listed in the paper in order to take a civil service test.

Using the quality times to prepare numerous of resumes, cover letters and monetary to get to these locations.

However, before going to fill out an applications or preparing a cover letter, it is best to know the qualifications of the positions, as well as any other opening the companies may have. If you can reach the company by phone, it is okay to ask questions about the pay rate, how many seats are open for that particular positions and if there are any other opening in other departments.

Many times CEO's will beat around the brush to avoid others from getting to a higher position. I know many of those before me, who had been on the job or in their field for years; doing the same type of work day in and day out and may had reach the salary cap (which are range between $40,000 to $47,000).

To play the game, you must first get your foot in the door. To have a solid step as you planted your foot unto the company ground. To assure that the company has a solid foundation, a secure future. Once you have that foot planted, the next step is to slide your arm in the doorway to reach out to those in higher level, to grasp a hold unto them in order to learn the step of becoming a successful employee. Like the old saying, "reach out and touch someone", but touch someone with vast superiority and well known by the communities. Then after that, is getting your body into the doorway. Being involved in the meeting, giving your output and ideas in helping your company grow and increase in better services for the communities. Being involved in the body will increase your recognition with other level executives. Afterward, is getting your head into the company. Becoming a master in knowing the business for the company, you worked. Such as knowing the procedure of how the company operates, knowing your employee's well-being and most importantly; knows the neighborhood around the company. Last is taking the other foot, placing it at a higher solid ground, as you persistently moves forward, were as at the same time with the other hand pulling someone else along the way.

However, back to the dirt, as I stated before to play the game you have to get your foot planted in the company. Communicate with your boss, get involved with your work, show anxiety for the customers, and get remarks from your customers and let them pass on the superior utterance concerning you. Get referrals from customers, in order to have other business under your belt, contact your CEO's and give your input (but not too much) to improve the business more in order to make the business grow. Yea, I know this may all sound B.S. but you have to play the game.

Have a union reps or someone in your defense or that will back you up when you in need of help. The reason why I said this is because many supervisors, managers and CEOs tend to avoid answering the questions, as well as seeing it as a threat to them as far as, losing money out of their pockets.

Many companies close out, due to bad managing, merging or companies filing for bankruptcy to protect their assets from the F.B.I (Federal Bureau Investigations) or I.R.S (Internal Revenue Services).

You must also understand that materials items can play a big role as well. You "the little people", as the big people called you, tend to go beyond your means. What I mean by this, you want to go and get the luxury cars, having the latest clothing and of course…jewelries. Then 'you' live either in the ghettos or in the projects. When will you ever learn that you have to live 'lean and mean'? What this mean is, by living lean is to be able to manage your money carefully; how you spend your money, in addition to, how well you save and invests.

Living mean does not stated to live being angry at the world (for those who may not know), but to live within your budget. If you choose to purchase something, it is wise to be sure, that it paid off in one lump sum. Avoid the monthly payment; due to the interest rates, you will be paying almost twice the amount of the item.

Don't Get Used;
But Learn How to Used It

Had you ever choose to work overtime on the job on a different assignment, because you want to make that extra money for whatever reason? I know many who had fallen in this hole and had gotten nowhere, even in their positions. Many people fall in this trap and get no respects at all, but a little piece of paper with a smiley face written; 'keep up the good work, job well done or great work'. The paycheck also shows how much time you work, with an even greater amount of being tax.

Too many people makes mistake of knowing exactly what their job is accordingly to their title. For example; let say if you were a porter (a person who clean floors); your job is to sweep, mop and bluff floors. Not bathe or feed patients, which are the nurse's job. On the other hand, if you are a bill collector, your job is to contact customers about paying over due bills, not to give out loans, that the finance department's duty. Everyone must know his or her roles as well as their responsibilities in this challenge work force.

Whenever you are filling out an application and whatever position you choose to desire for that certain company. If hire, it is okay to ask what are the roles and duties for that position. It is also best to write it down on paper to remind you, as well as protect yourself from doing others work that not listed as your job functions.

Know how to use the system, but do not over do it and never let the system string you into something that is against your will. If you are looking for that raise and choose to have more responsibilities added to your job function, usually it should take no longer than two week to know if your position will change, salary raise and the qualifications of the position that had to be met. If your position or salary does not change then you should return to your customary duties. Always think ahead of the game, know your next moves, and always prepare yourself for any oncoming reports.

You Do Not Need a
Degree to Be In the Field

How many of you went to college, graduated and had not gone in the field that you major in? Probably 80% of you have not even put your degree in play. I feel that students' need to litigate colleges, due to the lack of jobs fulfillment. Yes, many students do graduate from college and maybe they do put their degree in practice, but are they getting the right level of salaries that ought to receive. In other words, let just say that you are a registered nurse major and you are attending a two years college, paying close to $20,000 per semester. By the time you graduate, you should be making at least $30,000 to $40,000. Alternatively, let just say that you are attending a four-year institution, majoring in medical to become an orthopedic. Throughout numerous of years attending and paying for these courses, you might had paid over $40,000, then right after you graduate, you then have to attend another two to three years, paying an additional $20,000 to $30,000. So now, once you get in the career that you had study for so hard, will start you off around $50,000 to $60,000. This may sound great, but in reality, orthopedic starting paid is from $100,000 to $300,000. I know what you may be saying, 'people should love their career, and money should not be a factor'. Well in order to continue to exist in this world, you have to have money. So, to those who do not agree, then how are you going to get back and forth to work? How about having food to eat on a daily basic, clothes and the things, you want in life that gives the gratification and leisure that your sensitivity desire.

Do not fall in the trap of being string as a puppet. A degree, apiece of paper stated that you had the knowledge of the courses that you passed. A degree never stated that you have the skills or worked in the field two years or more. Many students make these mistakes when attending or about to graduate from college.

Once you had attended the college of your choice, while you are a full time student, it is wise to contact your counselor about getting in the field of your study. The best time to do this is when you are studying your major or usually when you are in your sophomore or junior year. Whether working as a part time employee or as an intern, at least by the time you graduate, not that you will have the knowledge, but you will also have the skills.

I, for my part knows those who had never attended college, but had been on the job for over four years and had to train new employees who just finish school. Now while the employee who had been on the job for over four years is receiving from $35,000 to $40,000. The new recruits from college receive an average of no more than $24,000. It is because the new recruits lack in the skills in their field. Look at Bill Gates, who is the Chairman of Microsoft; never step foot in college have a wonderful career and make tons of money. All because he had 90% of proficiency and 10% of understanding in getting his corporation widen. 'The more skills you have - the better paid you get'. Yes, knowledge is the key, but skills are the key to unlock to improved things in life.

The 'R' before the 'S' - Read before you Sign

It is very important to know what you are signing. It is also important to understand what written. Don't be afraid to ask question if you don't understand something, like my parent always tells me, 'a person who ask questions learns more than a person who don't ask at all'. When you do not ask about something that you are not able to comprehend, the other person will presume that you know what written or said. When you do ask question, not only will you get the answer, but your answer will be explain through example to make you understand better and more easier toward the question that had been ask.

Will you ever sign for a house that is worth $200,000, but the loan show very high interest rate, such as maybe 12% or how about property and school tax? In fact, your mortgage could have cost you about $1,600 a month, instead of $4,500 a month. Of course, you would probably reject the offer and research for a bank with a better rate and or you may decide to look at a different location. This is why it is best to appoint an attorney, who is willing to see that there is no lien on the house. Nevertheless, before all this, you have to do some milieu check of your own on the attorney that you may hire to help you go over any documents that you may not comprehend. Sometime reading is not always elementary. Words that written on document can make you full accountable for damages or additional secreted charges. Therefore, you have to watch out for those extremely careful and take your time in reading and understanding what you about to sign. Moreover, be certain what you paid or sign for, is the service you had or about to obtain.

Before signing for anything, you must carefully check for those fine prints. Remember, once you sign anything, it is like signing your life away. Therefore, bear in mind that even through everything maybe written in black and white, but there is always a gray area in between.

Learn to Save Your Money to Invest in Yourself

Different ethnicities have different ways of saving their money. Many save their money in a bank or in a safe at home. There are many reasons why people save their money. Some save up to get a car, some may save for a raining day, and others save to get more money.

I have seen many consumers who squander their money on products at a very high price, where in fact they can get the same products at a less significant price, if they only knew how to shop around for bargains. Let compare Costco (a warehouse full of varies merchandise) with either the Family Dollar store or The Dollar store itself. A plate in Costco of 125 counts may cost you $8.95, in The Family Dollar store; a count of 100 may cost you $1.50 and The Dollar store; a count of 100 may cost you $1. A $7.45 to $7.95 difference, the extra cash could be used for something else. The products are all the same, it just that the consumers are paying a higher cost, just for the name of the products. Let compare Martha Stewart's comforts to the Wal-Mart's comforts. In Martha's product only comes with a comfort that cost about $50 or better, where as in the Wal-Mart's comfort; comes with two pillow case, one sheet and a reversible comforts that will cost no more than $40. Both have the same quality, but different name.

I know many of you look for the quality of well-known name brand, but with the extra $10 or more can be a benefit in the end.

One-way and the best way to invest in, is yourself, you must invest in case of loss of job, accident, injuries or even death. Let see how you can invest to protect yourself and your love ones.

Many tend to go over their means when working, if the job is secure and stable. Well, the bad news is no jobs are secure or stable. The good news however, you can be securing your future, as well as being stable.

Many of those who go to church paid their tide, which is 10%. Well those that are so faithful in paying their tide should also be faithful in investing at least 20% of their salaries, bi-weekly for themselves. Not just putting money into your saving account; but also investing into mutual funds. A mutual fund is an open-end investment company that offers the investor the benefits of portfolio diversification (providing greater safety and reduced volatility), and professional management. The shares are redeemable on demand at their net assets value. The fund invests the pooled assets into various investment vehicles, including stocks, bonds, options, commodities, and money market securities. How the fund invests is determined by the fund's objectives. The mutual fund's prospectus details this type of information, along with a statement fee, a description of the management company, and other relevant data. A mutual fund that continually offers new shares and redeems existing shares is an open-end mutual fund.

It O.K. to be Guilty & Rich –
Then to be Innocent & Poor

In order to be successful in life, you have to take some chances and to get your hand dirty. How do you think people become multi-millionaires? By being nice…I think not. Sometime you have to step on toes or cutthroats just to get your hand in the goods. There are million and millions of rich folks out here in the world today that are making even more money, whether it is under the table or off the books. However, your government keeps telling you that the economy is in bad shape. Yea, bad shape in order for the government to raise the taxes, so that they can pocket more of your money. As the old saying, "the rich get richer and the poor get poorer".

Look around you; pastors are getting richer by the hour, while their members are still struggling to make ends meet; putting their trust in these bishops, pastors and traveling evangelists, yet they feel hopeless. Most pastors, bishops and these traveling evangelists makes millions and millions of dollars from offering, contributions, books selling and speaking at other functions. Yet, they less invest some of the funds back into the community or toward education, child care, health care and so forth.

There are only a few true pastors, bishops and traveling evangelists that I know and seen, that has given back and also help build up the community. To named a few:

Rev. Wade Richmond (retired pastor) from St. John Baptist Church in Arverne, New York, who help enlighten young men to become minister and encourage us that we can go beyond, outside of our community to help others and become leaders as well.

Rev. Joe Brown of Faith Baptist Church in Hempstead, New York; who help clean-up drugs within the neighborhood and encourage young men to get out of gangs and challenge them to avoid going to prison, to which the programs became a success

Rev. Floyd Flake (former Congressman of Queens, New York) pastor of, who open up a daycare center for single mothers, parenthood for first time mother and father; as a couple to administer and grow as a family

Rev. Grey of Mt. Carmel Baptist Church of Arverne, New York; who grew-up in the neighborhood, became a pastor and is still down to earth. He is level with the community as well as a true and straightforward preacher till this day.

The Late Pastor Jerry Falwell (founder of Liberty University in Lynchburg, Virginia), who help many students change their life around and challenge each and every students to spread the Word of God to those in need and trouble minded.

Act like the rich folks; avoid paying too much tax. Save your receipts, give to foundations or charities, and write it off for tax. Keep a log or record of everything you purchase. Remember, we get tax when we work, eat, where we live, car we purchase, clothes we buy and entertainment that we attend. Therefore, we are tax for everything, from the time we are born- to the time we are laid in the grave.

Final Solutions

Many companies' needs to be watch of how much revenues are being taken in compare to the employees salaries. Are the employees being paid fairly or is the companies on the verge of misinforming stockholders or just becoming more and more greedy? Since it is their company that has been started from their family members, does it give them the right to do what is outside of the law, but within the company's policy? It is illegal to hire an illegal immigrant, then to hire someone who may have the skills for the position, just to pay someone else for a minimum wage.

Many CEO's do deserve the paid they receive by having the reputation of their company, in keeping their company in a good and trustworthy standard. This is what also helps them to re-invest in their company to grow and to provide more open positions. By cutting back increase profits, but decrease in productivity; pressing other workers to reach their goals and increase in overtime paid. Therefore, one must understand how business work and how they used employees to great extend, showing little gratification of their hard work and keeping the company going. It doesn't matter how many years you may be on the job, if it take for them to cut you loose to save the business and it profits, they will do it with inexcusable reason. Many become successful without stepping in college, but in the long run if things fail, it may be wise to have one just in case.

Remember, before signing your life away, take the time to read and understand what you are about to sign. Avoid being trap in a contract or any misleading information. If you are unable to understand what you are about to sign, consult an attorney or someone you trust, so that it will not hurt you in the long run. Also understand to learn to save and invest your money; since having to work hard for your money, have those additional funds work for you.

Being guilty and rich can rid of many problems in your lives, then to be innocent and poor; worrying when the next check is coming in, bill collectors consent calling throughout the day and most of the night, while bills piling endless. It is O.K. to be a crook in this world. No matter what, when, or how you do it. It is legal, as long as you don't get caught.

Think smart, take your time, and always plan ahead.

THE WORLD WE LIVE

IN AS BLACKS

BY

John E. Farmer

'The world we live in as blacks, fighting against the whites in order to 'just have it', then having to come home in our own neighborhood, to fight an even tougher battle. What a Shame...'

'One finger may be pointing, but the other three are pointing back'

It All Start At Home

Yes, it actually starts at home. Many, young black men and women grow up with a single mom or grandmother; not getting the proper teaching of how to be a man or woman.

First, starting with the boys and the reason why I stated this black man a boy, is because the boy who is never raise by his own father will never become a man, unless that boy break the obstacle to be that man in raising his own seed right. Nevertheless, it is the duties for the man to be there whenever his seed(s) needed him for comfort and for acquaintance.

Now the little black girl who is taught at an early age of carrying around a white doll, treating the white doll with the utmost respect, compare to how a black doll is treated. In which the girl who tend to have her own at an early age, around 14 or 15 will never be a woman, due to not knowing how to hold onto that one man. In whom, she had her first child with. Nevertheless, the black girl will have numerous of kids with at least three or more different baby's father. This type of behavior is very un-lady-like and undesirable to the society as being seen as a hoar or someone to receives child support in order to avoid from working.

For a girl to be raise as a real woman she must have her parent and I mean both her mother and father.

Yet, let focus back to the white and black doll situation. The black girl is shown how well dress the white doll is, as well as the numerous of clothes, a big beautiful house with luxury furniture, a car and a baby with a white male doll. However, with a black doll, it is a completely different scenario. She is dress in other Caucasian's designer clothing line with a baby and no male doll. So, what this tells a black girl about her world and the white's world? She will take care of the white doll better than the black doll. Hun… you do not believe me. How many black women you know are nurses, CNA or RN? I bet more than any other professions. Whom do these black women mostly take care? I believe you get the ideal. It is ashamed that the black girls take much better care of the white patients than their own kinds. They are getting small paid for bathing, feeding, and other job functions.

'The way of who we are and who we become shows the way we respect each other, as well as how we want to receive the respect'.

So many young people today assume that the world owns them everything. It is up to the parent as well as the teachers and many adults in the community to advise the young adult, what the meaning of respect is.

Respect according to the dictionary, means to feel or show esteem for; to honor; Appreciation or willingness to show consideration.

Respects come accord to putting oneself in someone else's shoe and understanding the feeling of other.

So many little boys think that by having a flashy car or name brand shoe will give them the most respect. Even with rappers who think that coming with the best punch line, give them respect. Well it does, but only where they stand holding the mike and it does not even last long enough.

So all you boys and girls who think that you will receive respect without giving respect, well take a look into your future of those that are homeless for years and notice what respect they receive.

'Parents…it is up to you to stop the effects that are polluting our youth…in your own home'.

When I first stated that the problem started at home and how certain issue affects each and everyone of the black youth, it show the rate of crimes within our community. In every black neighborhood, drugs are the # 4 problem among the black youth. The first problem is at home; secondly, is respect/learning manners, and thirdly, is bodegas on every two to three corner blocks. Now to the fourth problem, which are the drugs in our communities.

Drugs do not force the blacks to kill each other. Regardless, if ones sold candy, car, or trying to receive some sort of business it all comes down to money. Money is the root of all evil, but it gets us the goods that we needs and wants. What really affect us is there are too many corner stores, which causes a hangout spot for the "street-pharmacy". By eliminating the corner store, can and will eliminate the risk of drug selling. Don't think so? At night between 7pm – 8pm, go to a white neighborhood and count how many corner stores there are. If any, are they open and I am not counting the 7-11 store. Count how many liquor stores are in or outside of the white's neighborhood. Notice how clean the streets are and the fresh crisp air compare to the blacks neighborhood.

'Live in my World or you will never understand me'

Living Standard

We as African-American people want to have a nice car, home, and a safe community. However, the ways in which black people live tend to downgrade themselves and only themselves. Blacks make themselves look insensitive when they mistreat each other. There are lacks of intelligence in the black's community. For example, why would you buy a $50,000 car and still living in the project/ghetto or worse still living with your parent? I mean it does not matter where you live, but what make it so imperceptive, is that the blacks with the luxury vehicle is either collecting welfare &/ living on section 8. What so funny about this; is the blacks who are in the pot, thinks that they are on top of the world or a ghetto superstar. Blacks have to change their attitude about one another, as well as having trust for each other. But what messed up blacks is too many little boys and girls sleeping with each other, no commitment, and when a child comes into this evil world, neither one are man or woman enough to take care of their responsibility. What is so ignominy is that the girl always assumes that the boy with the better living standard is the father of the child, where in fact, she has no idea who the father is, because of her slut ways? This is one of the reasons why there is a growing population of single mothers. This is one of the other reasons why there are so many bastards out here on the street; being born to live in prison. As I always stated to numerous of young boys, "If you think you are man enough to laid down with a woman, then you should be man enough to take care of that child" that you bring into this evil world. Moreover, for the girls, "if you think you are woman enough to spread your legs… then be woman enough to face consequence".

Blacks need to be concerned for their neighborhood; the smell of trash, homeless dogs and cats, young boys eminence in front of the store which can stop patrons from entering. This hurt business, which forces store's owner to raise prices.

Black's neighborhood can look as beautiful as the white neighborhood. Nevertheless, maybe the Caucasians are right about blacks; how lazy and uneducated blacks are. To end this dubiety about blacks on how blacks live, act, and communicate; blacks must educate themselves as well as bettering the community.

Many things within the black community have to be sacrifices, such as the corner stores, liquor stores and tobaccos. By eliminating these three problems, it can better the black communities at least by 70%. Why, I have not mentioned drugs and guns. In the white community, each home comprise an average at least 2 – 3 gun. Where as in the black household, average approx. 1 – 2 guns. Don't think this story is not true. A group of 10 to 20 members per gang, about five to seven guns are in the midst of them. Drugs on the other hand are bad. Nevertheless, will it be bad if the street pharmacy were to go into the white's community and make their profits off them. Then I guess it is worth being caught and going to jail.

It is the white men that drop off the guns and drugs to the young 'mannequin' black boys, who don't know any better? The white men get the easy money; while these young incomprehensible black boys continue to struggle to get by, sent to jail, or killing each other. These black boys are capable to merge, in order to open up a legitimist business, and bettering their community.

Therefore, I must not just blame the parents or the community; but I do blame the churches within the blacks' communities. How can a preacher preach about the problem within the community, where in fact, most of the preachers do not live anywhere near or within the community. The churches are not at the standard that it once was; instead of hoping & praying for someone off the street to walk in through their door, so called Christians are not reaching out to them. Churches should have programs for child care for those who are unable to afford, jobs assistance to help those in order to provide for their family, parent counseling to help young mother & father to cope with not just taking care of their child, but to work together and understand the commitment to each other and the understanding of marriage. Most churches do have programs in their community and they should be praise for what they are doing.

The church is the backbone of the community; they can have many negative sources push out of their neighborhood; such as strip clubs, liquor stores and or drugs. Can these causes be eliminated? Maybe not all, but at least their will be less crime, and less stress among the community.

'Parents need to take the time out for their kid(s), both at home and school'

Education

@ Home

Many parents tend to get upset at the teachers when the parent's child receives a bad report about their behavior, absentee, and level of their child(s)'s grades report. No teacher is looking to harm any child in any such manner. But, a teacher can discipline the child by first sending a letter home to the parent, as the letter can ensure the parent of a complicatedness that needed to be solved in order to correct the situation. If there is no response then usually the parent will receive a call, and if push come to shove, they; the teacher hope to meet with the parent one on one.

Education begins at home. It is primarily the parent responsibility in getting a head start for their child in learning, basic counting, and alphabets. This basic teaching should begin as early as 12 to 18 month. During this period, the child should also recognize shapes, as well as colors. In the black neighborhood, the child receives approx. 20% of knowledge within the home. Black mothers and father really need to take the time out to sit and educate their child, instead of looking for dates or how many partners they can sleep with. The games need to stop. The education that black receive the most is either from what is seen on television or violence video games. Education at home should be the most vital aspect in the black communities. Such as newspapers, news on television and writing about what is going on within the neighborhood.

Newspaper provides the source of knowledge of what is going on throughout the world. It is also a learning tool of writing, as well as how words are used to show the level of professionalism, and educational level.

A great way to practice reading is to 'READ'. Read the daily news or New York Times or any other local papers in your neighborhood, which are fills with large enormous amount of various writers. Sentencing that is created by verbs and adverbs show action as well as understanding. How they write for the readers to understand and by getting the picture of what the writer are writing about.

Today writing has become easier for those with trouble writing; in today technology, we now have computers with Microsoft Word that can find errors and make corrections.

The only time blacks will pick up a newspaper or book, is when an issue is about a famous black person, comic books, cars, motorcycles or half nude models; instead of what are assign to be read from their professors, something more meaningful in life or if a black author wrote the book.

At home, blacks have, what they believe knows everything and assuming of having a greater knowledge than anyone within what the community has. However, at home the qualify education that blacks have is being arrested on the media.

@ School

Secondly, are the lacks of education at many of our inner city schools. It is the teacher responsibility to get the black students the full attention of knowing what the real world is all about now and what blacks can learn from our history. I can remember when I was in the 8th grade, Mr. Rosario; my math teacher, who got the attentions of the students by letting us have fun in learning and telling jokes at the same time. Nevertheless, what was so special about this class was that, fifteen minutes before the class would end. He would take the time out to teach us college level mathematics. Any students that had this teacher learn a lot, not just advance math, but a few Spanish also.

Many teachers today just come in for the paycheck and it is ashamed for blacks that are receiving the lack of learning will become abortive in life. Many teachers tend to pass blacks, because of keeping blacks down at a lower level; putting into the mind of young blacks that they are only good in very few things, such as sport or rapping. They also encourage joining the armed service and low paying jobs. This is why black must persist to convert and edify one another to advance themselves to a superior and brighter secure opportunity.

'The World as I see it, will never change'

Thirdly, many blacks become skilled from the street. The way blacks become more of a vendor person, than any other professions. Blacks learn from what they see and how they look forward in a quick way to get money. Name brand clothing that are wore by the young blacks, such as Sean Jean, Fubu, Tims, etc., and spending their money on jewelry and luxury cars. Yet, with all this bling-bling, blacks scarcely pay their rent and utilities bills. What blacks learn from the street is to make money and spend money. This is not good at all when a black person have nothing stored for their future or children's expectations. What I also cannot understand is that the street; teaches blacks how to jostle and at the same time rob one another, which make no sense at all. What I cannot understand is that a nigger will steal or kill a black working man over nothing. Moreover, yes, a 'nigger' in other words, foolish by stupidly acts – not by color. Both men are in the same boat struggling to survive. What I am trying to make you, 'the reader' understand is why would a black man rob from one another and they both live in the ghetto, project, or within the same community.

The only one that the nigger is hurting is himself. Same for the gang members whose are born from the street and the educations they receive are becoming more-less skill for the real world.

Blacks will never succeed if they continue to receive the wrong information from the streets or niggers that have a negative outlook of the working world. This is why parents and teachers need to get more involve with the youth, to let them know that there is a better place within and beyond their neighborhood. The street does not teach the blacks about the history of black cultures. In fact, the street teaches poverties, lacks of knowledge, debts, criminal records, and high birth rates.

Blacks need to open their eyes and think outside the box. They must also be more knowledgably of what goes on in the world and show respect toward each other.

'A job ain't nothing but work!'
Marion Wayne-Mo' Money

Job or a Career

According to the eyes of the white Americans, they see that blacks are very lazy once they receive the job. After a few month of work, blacks tend to lessen their ability to push for a higher level. However, even when most blacks are posted or giving a higher position in their career, such as supervisory or managerial position; Blacks do less and less work, hoping to just be around for the next paycheck.

First, let talks about jobs and why blacks only look for job to just have in-between paychecks. Let define what a job is; a job is a temporary assistance of providing resources to, for, and by the public, in order to establish a lock-in within their environment. What I meant by this is that blacks are not motivated for a career. Oops! They do have careers, such as a street pharmacy, being on welfare, and getting on section 8. However, this comes with no retirement benefits. Conversely, some do get vacations – in an eight by six chrome bar with three meals a day, a steel plated bed, own personal lavatory and a small windowpane for a diminutive sunlight to come in. Oh and by the way, this vacation can last from six month to life and it all free! A job as many knows it as, 'Just Over Broke'.

It also is lowering the opportunity for blacks to enhance their skills for a government job, corporate/white collar job, or any jobs above the warehouse positions. What warehouse positions you may ask; how about assembly, clerical, packing, collection, or any position that halts you from interfacing with customers. I am not talking about retail store where you deal with customer service. I am talking about professionals.

Blacks work to spend more than what they can earn; they will buy things that they do not need and letting their bills continue to increase. Blacks also used job as a way to meet other employee for sexual interest or to bring other blacks down. Black hates to see other blacks have nice shit or trying to do good to improve for him or herself. This is why job is nothing but work and a waste of time for blacks to be involved.

Salary on the other hand, can play a major role to each individual as well as the community. How well maintain of the black life-style and outlook, depend on their routine.

Blacks do not know how to save or invest theirs money, because they are so caught up in glamour and luxury items. Everyday they spend their money like there is no tomorrow. The higher the salaries black receive, the more they go over their means. This is one of the reasons why blacks died poor and those that are left behind have to deal with the costs of funeral, burial, unpaid mortgage, and any unpaid taxes. The suffering goes from one generation to another.

Blacks also need to learn not to accept any positions that are thrown at them. For example, if you applying for an office position let say in a nursing/adult home. The first thing either a caucasian secretary or the interviewee will state that there is a open position in porter to sweep, mop, and bluff floor, or in the kitchen to cook or serve. Mostly, any positions that will try to keep black worker out of the public eyes in the work place.

I know personally, that caucasians does not have the qualification skills as the blacks. What gets the caucasians the top positions is the degree in the field of study, but cannot show the skills. While on the other hand, blacks have the skills, but what hold them back is not having the degree, and the black are the fool to show the Caucasian the skills in doing a certain task. But do not trust to show the skills to their own kind.

Blacks will not succeed in running a successful corporation, due to the fact of not helping and working together as one. Black are quick to jump out of their seat to help another race. I mean it nothing wrong helping other race, but there is no need to turn our back on our own blacks. Do the Jews help others? Maybe so, but they make sure that it will benefit their family, their own kind, and their community. I'm not trying to start a race war, but hoping to start a race challenge. I challenge the blacks to purchase from other blacks' clothing line and keep funding the growth within the community.

If any blacks believe that there is an equal employment opportunity, then they need to wake up and face reality. Go into a company with all white employees and see if you can get the job. You may be hire by the company due to the hidden law that every company has to have at least a certain number of minorities in the work place. However, as I stated earlier, 'they hire blacks for lower positions', but will blacks be hire for a more creditable position, like administration, manager, or chief executive office of a company. I am not talking about warehouse, garden, packing, or cleaning, this to me is unequal employment opportunity (ueo).

If blacks do not stand, more forward and stipulate the position and salary that they feel they deserves, then blacks will never get where they want to be. Blacks must be educated over and above getting the skills to get that position and the admiration they deserves.

'It takes money, to make money'

Managing Funds

Many blacks today have little or no money in the bank or in investment. Many excuses will come up about their indebts. Such as, I had rent to paid or I had kids to take care of. However, many have the money to purchase numerous of lottery tickets, a car they cannot keep up with payment, beers, liquors, and cigarettes. Blacks mistreat their money by punishing themselves. Buying unnecessary items that are not needed, like a big screen television, getting their hair done almost twice a week, and going to clubs spending their hold paycheck on over-charged drinks or slipping into the ladies' undergarment . They also have the predisposition to max out their credit card and then not able to pay it when the bill comes. They work hard for the company and too short for their money. For what, just to boast? Moreover, not letting their money works hard for them, I sometime just don't get it.

During this lesson, I will give a brief idea on how blacks should learn how to make their money work for them. Whether, blacks put their money in saving or investment.

Blacks need not to rely on sports or music to make money, but to learn to be patience when investing for their future in a long-term investment.

There are two ways to invest, according to my experiences. One way is to learn to control your money and the second way is investing in funds.

First, I will start with investing in funds. Two funds may be able to help you. One is a mutual fund and the other is the index fund.

A mutual fund is an open-end investment company that offers the investor the benefits of portfolio diversification (providing greater safety and reduced volatility), and professional management. The shares are redeemable on demand at their net assets value. The fund invests the pooled assets into various investment vehicles, including stocks, bonds, options, commodities, and money market securities. How the fund invests is determined by the fund's objectives. The mutual fund's prospectus details this type of information, along with a statement fee, a description of the management company, and other relevant data. A mutual fund that continually offers new shares and redeems existing shares is an open-end mutual fund.

On the other hand, an index fund is a large number of stocks packaged together where one can buy and sell them as a unit. Even through it sound just like a mutual fund, but it is different. It does not try to beat the market, because it is the market. It does not relied on mutual fund managers to buy and sell, but simply replicates the daily vicissitudes of how the stock market is doing on any given day (Wayne Wagner and Al Winnikoff, Millionaire, 2001 p.33).

Black need to trust and place their funds into Blacks owned banks, their may be none within one own community, however, there are plenty of unknown banks that are owned by Blacks, and yes, they are Federal Deposit Insurance

Carrier (FDIC). Even through, they may not be as large or popular as Bank of America or other well known bank in near your area, but why should we put so much trust in a bank that are owned by Caucasians and have second thought with those (blacks) who work so hard to assist us to have a better understanding of our moneys? Many Latinos borrows, invests and banks at their Latinos owned banks, and are being very successful at it. If they can do it, so can we.

'Before one can control it money, one has to control itself'.

Blacks have to sacrifice certain things in life in order to prepare themselves for the future.

'Hear me out!'

Communicating

Communication – what can I say about this? Well, it is the most vital information that is translucent from one living being to another living being. It is the most essential substitute of words and powerful at that - for blacks. Yet through, many blacks have so much to say, but just do not have the time to listen.

Crimes are cause through lack of communication. Blacks whose call out for help and those who tend to tune out the nature in which it endorses the blacks to be forceful through their own procedures; such as robberies or selling (according to the white men's law) illegal items.

Blacks used communication utterly different from how the caucasians communicate. Caucasians communicate through the court's system. They let the judge decide whatever problem or situation they may have. They also communicate through the value of knowledge; knowledge of knowing the law, whether it may seem right in ethics eye, but by law may show how wrong ethics may be. Knowing what is the best way for the two party to come to some form of agreement and they also make sure that the communication are met in writing.

Blacks on the other hand want to avoid the court system, not because they may had or have a record, but they are too obstinate to hear what the other party have to articulate, or they; themselves always assume they are 100% correct. With the lacks of edification and awareness, they become more jar-headed, as well as not making any sense at all.

Conclusion

The personal changes that had undergone recently were by isolating themselves from negative actions. Their reaction or effects of their distance from those who may need help, letting them know of a different direction and level that was heading for. The communities realize the change in time and knowing that they need to search for a change within themselves. Remember, it all begin at home; we as blacks need to change our living standard and to not just seek education at school, but at home as well… in order to avoid too much street education. We must have our mind set on career instead of just having a job. We must learn more of managing our funds and amplify our level of communications.

As far as my childhood, I'm in a different world now. My past community has worsen in education, more single parent develop daily within the community, more younger boys joining gangs because of the lack of fatherhood. Yet the leadership and the communities' churches, has slacken off and seeing blind of what's going on. I saw many things that I'd help change within the community, canvassing door to door, making changes in younger people lives for the betterment of the future of the community. The greatest momentous events in my life were speaking to a crowd of over a thousand voters in Philadelphia, Pennsylvania, during the Kerry's Presidential campaign. My speech was and has enlightened, empower, and educate the young people especially, explaining why it was important to register and to vote. This is what most trouble communities need, someone to sit down and communicate with them.

Overall, I just want to see African-Americans to improve theirs lifestyle, in every fields, not just sports or music, but from McDonald to being President of the United States.

The gap of our generations' lies between our ancestors and us, in which needed to be fill with the missing ingredients of:

Understanding who we are, understanding what commitment mean in a relationship, learning to build-up our community for the next generations and understanding the value of the dollar.

By having, a good understanding of each other can decrease the percentage of crimes and in reverse, increase the community to a healthier livelihood.

Many must and continue to understand that Africans that were slaves here in America build this country to what it is today, stronger and better with the increasing discoveries of America's future.

Black men need to detach the barriers of mistreating our black Queens, conflict upon each other, and the conscientiousness of our seeds. Therefore, let continue to climb and close the gaps.

THE 1ST MINORITY

PRESIDENT

OF

THE UNITED STATES OF

AMERICA

'WHAT HE/SHE MAY SAY AT THE INAUGURATION'

By

John E. Farmer

Behold, I will send my messenger, and he shall prepare the way before me: and the Lord, whom ye seek, shall suddenly come to his temple, even the messenger of the covenant, whom ye delight in: behold, he shall come, saith the Lord of hosts.

Malachi 3:1

As it is written in the prophets, Behold, I send my messenger before thy face, which shall prepare thy way before thee.

Mark 1:2

This is he, of whom it is written, Behold, I send my messenger before thy face, which shall prepare thy way before thee.

Luke 7:27

Universal Health Care

'Give me Health Care or give me Death!'

Choosing a health plan is an important decision. Universal health care is a health care system in which all residents or political entities have their health care paid for, regardless of medical condition or financial statuses. Universal health care systems do vary in what services are covered completely, covered partially, or not covered at all.

Health care for all American is vitality important. Diseases are form and discover every 8.3 seconds (according to Department of Health). In most countries that do have Universal Health Care are operated in a unique way. Where as the poor and the lower middle class, do not pay for any coverage. The coverage may be paid through the rich and upper middle class.

I believe that all Americans deserve to be and art to stay healthy in many ways:

1st is eating the right nutrition, with the proper breakfast of toast, eggs, grits with orange juice or milk; can help fight against cold virus, bone density and tiredness. However, in the opposite direction, it may help morning alertness.

2ndly, by having lunch helps keep the body fuel with energy and the mind focus. A good lunch can be anywhere from fruit, chef or garden salads with stream chicken or fish. Water or juices are also a great source of nutrition, but it best to shun from juices that are fill with sugar.

Moreover, for dinner such as: meats, vegetables, potatoes or rice, and juices or red wine (avoid the soda…too much sodium and acids which may cause outbreak of the skin). For those, who enjoy midnight snacks (like myself). Popcorn, unsalted chips, or peanuts are acceptable.

These are just my views on avoiding sickness and doctors visit.

But back to the Universal Health Care and how this system will work here in America for the American's people. First, let identify the percentage of coverage for the various classes. Starting with the children from birth to 21 years of age, should receive free health care at no cost [Parents that are in the lower bracket that are making a salary less than $25,000 (single) or $47,000 (married) with the same married name]. Married couple with different last name may have to pay [out of pocket] a small percentage.

Health care insurance has increase over 200% from 20 years ago, squeezing out the middle class. Reason for this is for couple that may have not be married or committed to ones health, which may disqualified their child(s), due to mother and father lack of health history, unable for doctors to perform any such surgery or decision making.

Children whose last names are the same as the parent shall receive free health care. However, Non-American or visitors to the States should pay 50% to 70% of their health coverage. Reason for this is that this program shall only be design for born American's citizen. Hard working citizens that paid their taxes and work for American's companies shall receive free health care services, from medications to dental care.

American universal health care's patients can be identifying in many ways: by their social security, birth certificates, or employment history.

Elderly should receive free complete health care, medications, dentals, or any emergency with no co-pay. I feel that the elderly deserves to be taking care of, for their many years of services here for the progress of the American economy. Publicly funded health care programs may help provide for the elderly, disabled, and the poor by ensuring public access to emergency services regardless of the ability to pay.

Universal health insurance would relieve the hassles and expenses of dealing with multiple health insurers. This may save over $500 billion in health care costs over 10 years. The goal is to bring coverage to those who may lack it in the next 5 years. This system can be financed through a mix of public and private contributions. However, the system can be primarily funded through tax revenue.

Here are the reasons why I believe there should be a support for universal health care:

- It ensures coverage to all citizens' in which can benefits a nation economically.
- Universal health care would provide for uninsured adults who may forgo treatment needed for chronic health conditions.
- With aligns incentives for investment in long-term health-care productivity, preventative care, and better management of chronic conditions.
- By providing access to medical treatment to those who cannot afford it themselves reduces

the severity of epidemics by reducing the number of disease carriers.

- This program can also encourage patients to seek preventive care enabling problems to be detected and treated earlier.
- Medical professionals will be able to concentrate more on treating patients rather than on administrative duties.

I want America to have the peace of mind that comes from having quality, affordable health care coverage that can be trusted. The people should have the freedom; to choose their own doctor(s), free annual physical exam, vision, dental checkup, and free annual routine hearing test.

Education

'I was always told that education is the keys, but I have not been giving the key to enhance my educations.'

As each and everyone know, education is very important for the level of knowledge in the structure of the world in the growth of life.

Many of our children are not receiving the quality educations due to overcrowded classes, lacks of attention and lack of entertainments within the community.

I believe that schools should be extended an extra hours and an extra month. I feel that student athletes should attend classes in the morning, while non-student athletes attend mid or late afternoon classes.

Future teachers should be able to volunteer their time in helping those that are falling behind in their classes. Better program need to be develop, such as after school program, 2 hours morning session on Saturday and practice test taking.

According to the Census Bureau, the percentages of graduate are dropping. More and more students are dropping out to help support family or siblings. Our government had failed the communities and the school's system as a whole. Teachers being underpaid, programs being taken away due to the lack of funds, classroom being packed like livestock and schools are under funded.

I believe that the government, before any of the newer school receiving any funds, should first fund present schools. This step is what keeps the original schools open in the lower middle class neighborhoods. In which will help lower the overcrowding of the newer schools and keeping tracks of the funds that are being distribute to various schools.

Teachers risking their lives every school's day in the classroom dealing with agitate students, intercede in fights among students and covering additional non-positions due to the lack of finance of hiring staffs for opening positions. More and more programs being cut off create an increase in the dropout rate. Programs are what keep the mind alert and encourage students to reach their potential goals. By adding more fun, safe and educational programs may eliminate the crimes in our communities. In order to eliminate overcrowding classroom, school's hours must be extended, where as it can open doors for additional position. This I believe will help students focus more on their subjects and be more active in a positive mind in class.

The quality of our children's education is the results of America's future.

Funds from Gambling

'Gambling is the way to solve problems'

Casino avenged around $90 billion dollars per year. However, outside of the casino's perimeter (ex. Atlantic City), the neighborhoods are crippling and being overlooked. Taxes going up, schools suffering from lacks of fund and hard working taxpayers are losing their home. There must be a change for the better.

I believe a percentage of funds from each casino can help the economy development; providing affordable homes, cut in taxes and lower the cost of health care.

With the small spending, states will not have to depend fully on government spending. Funds being channel into troubling neighborhood may create jobs and job training for local companies.

Schools that are in need of funds can cut education cost about 20% and more teachers can be hires (on a part time basis) for after school program, to help those that is having difficulty learning in class. We also definite need to save the homeowners, with gambling; it can benefit the reduction of property tax, school tax, and homeowners to be able to keep their home. Gambling funds can be great benefits for many lacks of funds that need to be plug. I believe it may also lessen public assistance. I feel that there should be a temporary public assistance for those that are not permanent disable. It may help those to get back on their feet, in, which can also help lower taxes for the taxpayers.

I just not focusing on casinos, to fund the state that they operate in, but Lotto's and online betting sites are in needs to take part as well. Lottery money that were suppose to go toward schools and then transferred money that were spend on schools to cover other parts of the state budget is called lottery shell game. I will end this shell game by spending the lottery proceeds directly on general state aid to school districts and other educational programs.

By expanding gambling can generally be a benefit for all states. Each state may receives about $700 million annually from gaming revenues. With the ability to know what revenues from gambling would be, then the state should be able to match expenditures to keep them in line with what the gaming generated.

For example: let say, your property tax is $4,000 per year and school tax is $2,000 per year. Making a total of $6,000 per year in taxes and let say, you gamble $2,000 in a year using the comp card that the casino provides to patrons. The government should be able to exempt at least 50% of what you gamble at the casinos. However, only if you use your comp card, which may only be deducted only from playing slots machine. Table games, horses or sports betting, or dining will not be included. Therefore with $1,000 being deducted, $500 may be deducted from school tax and $500 deducted from property tax.

How can this be identifying? One is by filling out a form(s) that should be issue by the federal government. Providing comp card number, the name, and address of the casino(s) that patrons gamble for verification (only within the state where the patrons live). This type of program can only take effect within the state of resident and gambling casinos. Gambling in another state or non-residents will be voided.

Same for lotteries, by saving non-winning tickets, may also help in deduction of only school taxes, in which patron may be deducted up to $500 per year. This system is mainly for homeowner(s) who do paid property and or school taxes.

Armed Services to Accept All American

'Uncle John wants YOU!'

I, for many years tried to join the armed service and been denied, passed the test and all physical in which I was and still is in top shape and better shape than most service forces that are already in the service, due to one thing and that was my hearing (actually from one ear), in which anchor a struggle in the workforce.

I believe that this policy and procedure of joining the service should change. I feel that all American should be qualify to be in the service, unless if one fails more than two physical and they must be major or permanent conditions. If the problem(s) can be fixed, then the applicant may be accepted. Without having to go through the whole process, the applicant will just be tested only for the test(s) (reading, math, and or physical) that it fails. Yet, those applicants with minor problem may serve no less than 2 years before receiving full military benefit. With this change, it may help improve Homeland security, strengthen our military, and fortify our border patrol.

Our military and the involvement of both American men and women, is what keep America alive. If we continue with the procedure of military joining; then our military will dwindle over the years, and will become very vital to other countries. We must grow in great number and strength to still be the superpower Nation.

We also need to fully take care of all our American's troops and ensure that their families are compensated as well.

Saving our American Men from Prison

'An injustice system is a prejudice
system for the black men'

Prison is one of the reasons why our taxes go up. It is not the lack of education, no father, or role model in these young boys lives, but the lack of activities. What I meant are jobs. I feel with the right training and motivation will lower the crime rate and our taxes. With border-patrols in high demand may tighten our border from illegal immigrants who illegally entering our country. On the other hand, punishment needs to be stricter on both sides.

Biases of race and poverty saturate the American justice system. African-American men are nauseatingly over-represented in prisons. Every Black male child grows up with a sense of his chances in life. In many places, a young Black man is far more to be expected to go to prison than to college. According to the Department of Justice, the rate of African American men in prisons is approximately 10 times greater than 30 to 40 years ago.

The effects on minority communities are intense. Imprisonment shatters families, racially biased police stops strain neighborhoods, and ill treatment terrorizes people in our cities. When prisoners re-enter our community, they enter without housing or jobs, denied supports to re-establish themselves emotionally and economically. Being left in poverty, what are our Black men to do?

There was an article by Stanley Crouch who is a writer on, On Culture of the Daily News. What capture my attention was the title stating: Memo to young black men: Please grow up. Within his statement that was written states this and I quote: Those who believe that America is perpetually adolescent will point at the dominance of frat-boy attitudes among successful white men and will say of black hip-hop generation, "So what? How could they not be adolescent? They are not surrounded by examples of celebrated maturity. The society worships movie stars, wealthy athletes and talk show hosts. These are not the wisest and most mature of people."

Hip hop began as some sort of Afro protest doggerel and was very quickly taken over by the gangster rappers, who emphasized the crudest materialism in which the ultimate goal was money and it did not matter how one got it. The street thug, the gang member, the drug dealer and the pimp became icons of sensibility and success, then the attitudes of pimps took a high position and the pornographic version of hip hop in which women become indistinguishable bitches and hos.

These young black men do not see growing up as having any advantages to it. The only success they think they can believe in is had by either athletes or rappers. Young black men. So they hold on to adolescence and adolescent ways as long as they can.

They identify with the overgrown boy, who is everywhere and who is getting over. He's got a lot of cash, plenty of girls, lots of jewelry, an expensive car. To them, that's the world. Or it's the world they want to be part of.

From one end of the country to the other, adults sleep in the street for nights on end as through they are homeless in order to have choice places in line when PlayStations go on sale. That alone gives us more than an indication of how great a problem we find ourselves facing. End quote.

Solutions

Having Universal Health Care will have a positive impact on many American lives, especially for those who may not be able to afford it. Not having to worried of being sick, knowing that they can get the treatment that is needed. Insurances will be more affordable and less hassle for the insurance companies and medical facilities' billing department.

Education is the key for all American and should at some point be mandatory for students that finish high school, be giving at least one year of free college's education, which may enhance our country and decrease both poverty and crime levels.

Funds from gambling should be able to cover most taxes within the community as well as education. It should also assist in property taxes, which may have an impact on the market values on the homes that casinos are located in and or how often people gamble within their community at their favorite local store.

Our military are what we American heavy depend on, keeping America and human lives around the globe, in general to be free; to protect humans' right and equal justice for humanity.

In order to decrease the level of men in prison is to provide on-the-job training and job that will accept them regardless of past-history. If companies are more open to-not just providing the position, but also the necessary paid-rate, then we can cut down on crime and the corporations that are accumulating millions and millions of dollars off the back of prisoners in these private prisons.

Yet, we as an American need to produce more and more kept and stable job here in the homeland, instead of being oversea. We as an American need to be more and more dependent on our own resources than to consume and rely on foreigner's imports. I feel, in my own opinion; since we American have more foreigners and/or immigrants, coming into America. We should be able to either tax them (foreigners/immigrants) at a higher tax-bracket or depending on the percentages of those coming from various countries; that their countries should give us (American) the necessary resources, due to the fact of their citizens consuming up our sources here at home. This may be agreeable to some and not a good idea for others; however, in order for America to be the superpower that we are claim to be, then we must show it not through military, but through our own produce resources, without relying on others.

DIGGING FOR BLACK GOLD

'TO DRILL OR NOT TO BE DRILLED,
IS THE FUTURE THAT WE MUST FACE'

By

John E. Farmer

Allies or Self-Dependences

Exploring oil for America may be a challenging issue for the Government to decide when and where to drill, and the impact it may have on the American people. Deciding to rely on self or other for oil, to either drill onshore and or offshore. America needs a balanced, fact-based energy policy that promotes energy efficiency and conservation and greater supplies of all forms of energy.

The impact on America's search for oil depends on whose land to drill, others countries or our very own.

Getting oil from other countries such as Iraq, Saudi Arabia, and others; costs the American's taxpayers more and more to have the oil developed, stored within the refinery, shipped to the United States (U.S.) coasts, delivered to local oil companies and last delivered to local gas stations. There are probably further measures of getting oil here to the U.S. America currently imports more than 55% of the oil that it uses. However, if the U.S continues to depend on foreign oil, prices will continue to rise as more and more immigrants become U.S. citizens, increasing the amount of oil used daily, and of course the used of oil during the winter month.

There is plenty of undiscovered natural gas in the U.S. beneath the land owned by the federal government, such as Alaska, Texas, Utah, and many other federal protected lands. The government owns 657 million acres, which is approximately 30% of the U.S. land mass. If the oil companies actually went ahead and drilled on all of the land currently available to them, it would generate an additional 4.8 million barrels of oil a day, which would nearly double the amount of oil produced within the U.S.

The challenges in costs depend on where the oil is coming from, most believe that it is better and cheaper to drill on our own land than to receive from far-away land; which may also cause an effect of drilling onshore and or offshore. Onshore, there are 47.5 million acres of federal land leased by oil and gas companies, and those companies are drilling on 13 million acres (34.5 million acres unused). Offshore, there are 44 million acres of land leased by oil and gas companies, but they are only drilling on 10.5 million acres (33.5 million acres unused) and are still unable to keep up with the demand of oil. Futures contracts obligate buyers and the sellers to purchase or deliver crude oil more months in the future. However, delivery of crude oil rarely occurs in conjunction with futures contracts. The difference between the contracted future price and the actual cash price when the futures contract comes due, or expires; is usually settled in cash.

Secondly, due to shortages in crude oil supplies, there is consideration to develop the vast petroleum resources located just outside of our outer continental self's. Drilling onshore and or offshore may be a great option to cut costs and create faster delivery on-demand. There may be less weather and terror threats, and mid-range security in protecting the drilling ports closer home than oversea.

There may be some effect in the long run, while on the other hand, there is always a risk if giving the potential of oil drilling. The concern of most American people is the drilling site; will it causes noise or air pollution, and extraction of natural resources, and the economic impacts?

The Effects

The environmental impacts from drilling range can disrupt of wildlife reproduction, their habitat, basic life function, and population morality. Drilling may pose a danger of waste disposal being mishandle, accidental spills, rupture, and leaks. It can also effects the air quality from the injection pumps, that pumps smoke into the atmosphere and soil erosion or loss of land due to drilling. If oil gets out in the opening or in harms way of the environment, it will have a big impact on the eating patterns, reproduction and life span.

On the economic, having oil is one thing. Delivering it to a growing market is another. America economics differ greatly in their capacity to organize enterprises, adopt new technologies, raise capital and supply what consumers want. When it comes to increasing oil production, economic systems matter. More oil would flow onto the markets and prices would be lower if major oil resources were in countries where producers responded freely to market incentives. The extent of economic freedom in the countries with the world's oil supplies will greatly affect how well the oil is delivered to consumers. The economies of the U. S., other major industrial nations and the newly industrializing countries have continued to grow. They've withstood the price shock because greater energy efficiency has made them less dependent on oil and supplies have risen to meet increasing demand.

The public is also concern of the problems they may face. The main concern is the contaminated food and water, from accidental leaks or spills being the primary threats to the human's health. The human health pose a greater risk from the levels of air pollution generated from the drilling operations, which released chemical toxic into the earth atmosphere, even with low pollution levels. The toxic in the air may affect the central nervous system, respiratory failure, and cancer-causes.

Thirdly, can we find the solution to decrease the rising problems that America is facing? Yes, by providing consumers with rebate and tax incentives; for the purchase of energy efficient appliances and the constructions of energy efficient buildings and rebates, for the installation of renewable energy generation equipments.

Will the solution work and are we taking the step to find the resolution in oil drilling that will not harm the environment and human health?

Taking the necessary steps in maximize the protection of environment, retailers, refiners of petroleum products, users of explosives, and the public in the areas, will help design a safe awareness of ensuring a better and less hazardous drilling process. The protection of public health and the environment from contamination caused by leaking petroleum storage tanks and prevention of releases from all regulated storage tanks. Each drilling and servicing company has its own safety program. Safety awareness is necessary for injury prevention during all phases of drilling and servicing operations. Procedures include safety meetings, and general and task-specific training.

Working in a New Direction

So what are the latest ways to go? The 'Green' way, safer and cleaner, such as Biofuel, this produced from photosynthetic plants that capture solar energy. Many different plants and plant-derived materials are used for biofuel manufacture. The production of biofuels to replace oil and natural gas is in active development, in the efficient production of liquid and gas biofuels, which yield high net energy gain. One advantage of many biofuels over most other fuel types is that they are biodegradable, and so relatively harmless to the environment if spilled. Biodiesel is made from vegetable oil. Biogas produced by the biological breakdown of organic matter in the absence of oxygen. Biogas originates from biogenic material and is a type of biofuel. One type of biogas produced by biodegradable materials such as manure or sewage, municipal waste, and energy crops.

Bad things about going green are the cost. Natural and organic products are 25-30% more expensive than their counter products. Take ethanol, for example: it is not any cheaper to produce, it takes 5 gallons of regular gas to produce one gallon of ethanol. The plants, where ethanol is produce drastically pollute the surrounding areas, lowering the values of properties in the nearby towns/cities. The pollution from the ethanol refining plants is actually much worse than from the pure gas fuel and raises the prices of food. One of the largest offshore areas in the U.S. with shallow water is off Cape Cod, where a major wind farm has been proposed. Much of the rest of the U.S. coastline has at least some potential for wind development, but typically, turbine foundation costs increase rapidly with increasing water depth and wave height. The cost of connecting with utility power lines also increases rapidly as the distance from shore increases. Population growth and urban development worldwide continue to increase the use of fossil fuels, such as oil, coal and natural gas, which emit carbon dioxide and other gases into the atmosphere. At the same time, the clearing of land for agriculture, including deforestation, is releasing carbon dioxide into the air and reducing carbon uptake by the biosphere.

In Conclusion, as our economy grows, producing greater wealth and technological innovation, oil and natural gas companies and other businesses will find better, more cost-effective ways of reducing emissions. The industry has proven it can safely develop oil and natural gas resources in all areas, including federal lands. With new technologies, the industry has and will continue to reduce the environmental footprint of exploration and production by drilling fewer wells to access greater amounts of production.

Production of oil and natural gas on federal lands has brought billions of dollars of revenue into federal and state treasuries. Oil and natural gas are vital to our energy and economic future, where as, America needs a balanced, fact-based energy policy that promotes energy efficiency and conservation and greater supplies of all forms of energy. The less America depends upon foreign oil, the less vulnerable we are to terrorist attacks that could dramatically affect the American economy.

It has been argues that more drilling for gas deposits on federal lands will do little to answer long-term energy challenges in the U.S. Pitfalls of more drilling on public lands; Increase in the drilling activity throughout the country; Views on the efficiency of the national energy policy.

Expresses views on the issue of whether U.S. Congress should allow more drilling for gas deposits on federal lands. Cause of the tight supply situation in the gas market; it has been views on the issue of natural gas shortage; in spite of the sufficient gas reserve legal barrier to oil and gas development in the country.

First, the Impact of America in a positive as well as a negative factor on oil; according to what I had recorded from various meeting and discussion among local and state government will show the debate and how it may change each and everyone livelihood.

The impact on activity and demand in the United States and euro area are somewhat larger than the industrial country average, while the impact on other industrial countries is smaller than the average, because the largest two members of this group such as the United Kingdom and Canada which are net oil exporters. The financial impact of the increase in oil prices is quite muted. Exchange rates remain relatively stable, with the dollar appreciating slightly relative to the yen and euro because the United States faces a smaller terms-of-trade shock.

The impact of higher oil prices on growth and activity in oil producing countries will depend on a variety of factors, most importantly how these windfall oil revenues are spent. In many oil exporting countries, a significant proportion of higher oil revenues will accrue to the government. The reaction of the government, in turn, is likely to depend on the underlying financial situation of the country. Saudi Arabia, which has traditionally been a net creditor, may choose to replenish reserves. The authorities may also decide to use some of the additional revenue to ease spending restraints adopted as oil prices declined. For other oil exporters that have in the past been net debtors, such as Mexico and Venezuela, a rise in oil prices would not only increase export earnings but could also lower external borrowing costs, assuming the higher oil prices would reduce the risk premium charged these countries as their future export earnings rose.

The negative effects in my opinion, mining and oil operations can have serious economic implications on America. Large projects attract economic migrants, place heavy demands on municipal services, and stress local government agencies.

In general, mining and petroleum projects are capital-intensive, not labor-intensive. Purchases by companies working in local areas are minimal, as global companies bring in supplies from other regions and even overseas. Although an oil or mining company sometimes invests in local school programs and other services, these benefits must be weighed against the environmental damage and negative health effects the community suffers long after the mine or oil well is abandoned and the company pulls out. Oil exploration is a specialized activity, and if wells are drilled, they do not require very much labor from the local work force. Many governments suffering from unsustainable debt must rely on oil and minerals exports to pay back loans from international financial institutions. The negative effects of mining and oil drilling are not always fully examined when such loans are considered—and cash-strapped governments are not always inclined to consider other options.

Secondly, my preparation on debating both the positive and the negative sides of onshore and offshore drilling, is the impact it may have on our environment and the benefit that we may occur in self dependence.

The positive aspect of onshore drilling is the cost will not be high; it will take less travel time to stored, refined and distributed to local stations, requiring hundreds, if not thousands, of acres of large tanks, refineries, roads and rail lines. Concurrent with this is the constant stench of petroleum and unbelievable light pollution. As far as offshore drilling, the drilling rig would not be visible from the beach, having newer technology which is safer than ever before, that are able to extract at least 420 trillion cubic feet of natural gas – fifty to a hundred miles offshore.

Yet, when there's a positive, there's a negative reaction to onshore and offshore drilling. Study was conducted to identify potential environmental effects that could be uncured if such drilling were allowed in the US. Currently, onshore and offshore drilling, and production access oil beneath our states, but not beneath our lake or rivers. Any new onshore development of oil and gas systems beneath the lakes would likely be conducted in a manner and may be expected to utilize existing infrastructure for the transport and refinement of the oil and gas extracted from beneath the Great Lakes. The primary environmental effects of accessing oil and gas systems beneath and adjacent to the lakes or rivers would be associated with the following: The potential disturbance of ecological and/or cultural resources during exploration and the construction of the well site; Exposure of biota, sensitive habitats, and areas important for tourism and recreation to accidental spills or releases; and, to a lesser extent, the visual and noise intrusion of oil and gas developments on areas that support recreation and tourism.

But the greatest concerns are for accidental releases that may affect wetlands, unique habitats, fishes, and aquatic birds.

Spills may also affect recreational activities, consumption bans for fish and game, and affected land and water use. Impacts to these resources would also involve the loss of use while the spill is being addressed. With the exception of very large spills, impacts to land and water use for most spills may be expected to be localized and minor. However, depending on the location of a spill and the proximity of a water intake structure, short-term but significant impacts on public drinking water supplies may occur. These are the same spill-related concerns that exist for current oil and gas production activities in our water Offshore development may result in more environmental impacts and effects more than Onshore development, because offshore wells would require both offshore as well as onshore infrastructure to collect and process the oil and natural gas. Thus, offshore development would involve a greater level of disturbance of both terrestrial and aquatic resources during construction. In addition, offshore spills in open water would be more difficult to contain and may affect a broader area than an onshore spill.

Third is what we should do to become greener and what we shouldn't do to avoid high cost. Wind turbines can be sited offshore, where the wind blows harder and larger turbines can be installed. Many offshore wind farms are being proposed and developed today in densely populated Europe, where there is limited space on land and relatively large offshore areas with shallow water. However, the urgent need to respond to climate change means that we will need to use as many renewable resources as we can, as quickly as possible, and that means both onshore and offshore wind. Also, the U.S. has very large onshore areas that are suitable for wind development, and not so much suitable offshore area. Still, there are advantages to sitting wind farms further offshore. Wind speeds tend to be higher and the wind is steadier. Wind turbines outside of established shipping lanes, thereby avoiding conflicts with routine traffic. Should a ship inadvertently go off course, its radar will readily detect the wind turbines, which are excellent radar reflectors. Wind turbines are also equipped with warning devices to alert ships in foul weather. The U.S. Coast Guard authorizes wind turbine locations for navigational concerns and determines the markings, lights, and fog signals.

Furthermore, since many people like the look of wind turbines, it should not be assumed that it would be more desirable to put all wind turbines far offshore. Onshore wind farms can provide significant economic development in the form of tax revenue to hard-pressed rural communities and rent payments to farmers. Onshore wind farms can therefore make a significant contribution to reducing and reversing the decline of rural communities that we have seen in the Plains States over the last several decades.

On the biggest of all issues, climate change, Companies aren't changing quickly or significantly enough to move the needle. And in some areas, things are getting worse. Electronic waste more than doubled between 2000 and 2005, for example, despite all the good work that Dell and HP have done around recycling. Although the organic food industry is booming, the 2002 USDA census of agriculture— the latest data available—found that only 0.14 percent of acreage in the U.S. is farmed organically, and pesticide use was higher in 2005-2006 than in 1999 or 2000.

The report, which can be downloaded at www.greenbiz. com, is a must-read for anyone interested in green business. It reports on 20 indicators including macroeconomic measures, such as carbon emissions, toxic releases and paper use per unit of gross domestic product, as well as business-specific measures such as corporate fleet purchases of alternative fuel vehicles, construction of green office space and investments in clean tech.

Finally, the study doesn't attempt to measure either political or cultural attitudes about business or the environment. By saving the environment - keeping it clean and healthy - we preserve our own health. Many of the un-green products that harm the environment also harm you and me. The good intentions that some companies have made in efforts to reduce energy and waste; by cutting emissions and invest in clean technologies. Companies are getting cleaner, and more efficient, but only incrementally, and many of the gains are offset by the ever growing economy in a new report called the State of Green Business 2008, produced by, Greener World Media.

Cutting back on newspaper delivery is the next step. The purchases of alternative fuel vehicles, construction of green office space and investments in clean tech.

Solutions

The claim and corresponding that I believe is most unique is the funds that it may take to go green. It will cost the taxpayers even more money to produces ethanol in order to have cleaner air. It will cost companies to raise the price of oil in order to build upgraded factories and biofuel machine, to convert corns into oil, which can take a longer process to produce. It will also affect the farmers having to increase the price of corn, to give up at least 25% of their crops for alternative fuels. It will also be a bearing to produce feeds for their animals as well. As stated previously, that natural and organic products are 25-30% more expensive than counter products, which cost more to ensure that the products are not mist with any chemical. The purchases of alternative fuel vehicles may cost even more to reengineer the motor, mixing alternative fuels with either oil or water along with the air input in order to ensure the rpm output and the lasting of the vehicle. Turning government building in construction of green office space will also fall back on the taxpayer's pockets.

The least concern will be getting oil from other countries; which will cut the costs of the American's taxpayers from having oil developed, stored within the refinery, shipped to the United States (U.S.) coasts, delivered to local oil companies and delivered to local gas stations. Whereas the American will not have to worry about onshore or offshore drilling, that may harm the environments or our health. There'll be less weather and terror threats that occur in other countries and the ocean. There will be less Mid-range security in protecting the ports closer home than oversea. There'll be lesser concern of the American people on drilling site; the causes of noise or air pollution, and extraction of natural resources. It will also be a less concern depending on other countries or the price they charge us and won't have to worry about the control of importing oil; in reverse we can start exporting ethanol as a way to pay off our debts.

My strongest case in supporting my topic is 'Going Green' is not all that great. It can be a huge affect on the taxpayers and cost businesses even more money to become and to stay green. The media tried to raise awareness of the changing earth climate or the decrease in the wildlife, to have the public to change its ways of how one lives. Yet, they the media don't tell how it can affect the pockets of the taxpayers. It will cost even more to install energy-efficient products within our home, business and the vehicle that we drive. Which mean that those business that choose to go green, will have to change their lighting to energy saving, home owners installing solar panel, oil companies converting corns into ethanol and grocery store providing organic products to change the way we eat. Yet, all this will cost almost double the amount to make these changes and to manage.

Going green may improve the health of the American people, but it will not decrease the amount of fumes in the air that comes from airplanes, ships and space shuttle that are launch into space almost every quarter of the year and is continuing to increase. Greedy entrepreneurs and businesses are taking advantage of the growing appetite for clean technologies. Overcharging organic products and investing in stocks that are green technology, all for the sake of the Arctic Circle (polar bears, melting ice, etc.).

It is a shame how people wanting to change and control other people lives. The government with-out looking at the outcome, seem to side with complainer to choose to add more taxes on tobaccos and alcohols assuming that it will get the public to cut back or quit smoking or drinking. Tobacco could become the new drugs, if taxes continue to rise. Therefore, going green is not all expected to be great… there is some downfall and that downfall is the cost.

The reason why I believe that going green is not all that great, in response of providing the evidence are shown as follow: A written book called, The Clean Tech Revolution: The Next Big Investment Opportunity, which show how businesses can follow the lead of companies such as Toyota to go green and make green dollars. A report on "Good Morning America", Wal-Mart also is going green to installing skylights, fluorescent light bulbs, more efficient trucks, but didn't mention any upfront costs associated with making the green changes and is the costs going to fall back onto the community. How about FedEx, which uses clean burning hybrid trucks, won a prize in 2004 from the Environmental Protection Agency – yet fail to state that the hybrid trucks cost 75 percent more than regular trucks.

We must understand that the earth is billions of years old. I find it extremely arrogant that we (humans) could be the downfall of this planet. Going Green is mainly a marketing ploy for companies to present newer products. Corporations in my opinion have falsely advertised practices that they have utilized for decades unnoticed. The media and government makes most people think that we have caused a global warming epidemic everyone has become self-conscious of their energy consumption. People are responsible for global warming; people need to realize that any effort at the reversal of such an effect is pointless. The media and most 'Green Activist' may not convince enough individuals to participate in the actions that it would take to reverse any warming trend, we may have created. It is important to realize this because currently this is wasting valuable life time and resources, trying to convince people of this trend instead of accepting that it's not a trend but unavoidable.

For example, the fires that had occurred in southern California are proof that nature will take care of itself. The arrogance of humanity mystifies me. The earth is no longer a life birthing planet and the species is has given rise are merely parasites now. We have adapted to a given environment and will continue to do so as much as we possibly can. However, when "Mother Earth" decides to abort us, that's it, no matter what action we take in an attempt to conciliate the environment.

After reviewing the differences of drilling for oil and going green had shown, that no matter which way we may choose to head, there's always going to be a good with the bad. I consider this composition to be strong in the following areas: First, should America continue to obtain oil from foreign countries; Secondly, American should begin to seek it own oil on its own land; Third, the conservation of natural resources and wildlife; Fourth, is it ok to Go Green; and Fifth, the effect on the taxpayers.

Getting oil from other countries may costs the American's taxpayers more and more to have the oil developed, stored within the refinery, shipped to the United States (U.S.) coasts, delivered to local oil companies and last delivered to local gas stations. There are probably further measures of getting oil here to the U.S. America currently imported. However, if the U.S continues to depend on foreign oil, prices will continue to rise as more and more immigrants become U.S. citizens, increasing the amount of oil used daily, and of course the used of oil during the winter month.

Drilling for gas deposits on federal lands may be a great option to cut costs and create faster delivery on-demand. More drilling on public lands throughout the country may cause America to pay lower taxes and less dependences for oil across sea, which may be the answer of long-term energy challenges in the U.S. With less weather and terror threats that occur in other countries and the ocean. There will be less Mid-range security in protecting the ports closer home than oversea.

The potential conservation of natural resources and wildlife may effects, if such drilling were allowed in the U.S. Most are weighed against the environmental damage and negative health effects the community may suffer long after the mine or oil well is abandoned and the company pulls out. However, the greatest concerns are for accidental releases that may affect wetlands, recreational activities and games usage.

Going Green is focus mainly on energy saving, converting corns into ethanol and organic products. By saving the environment - keeping it clean and healthy - we preserve our own health. Many of the un-green products that harm the environment also harm you and me. The good intentions is that some companies have made an efforts to reduce energy waste; by cutting emissions and invest in clean technologies. Going green may improve the health of the American people and their way of living.

The effect on the taxpayers may cost almost double the amount to make these changes and to manage. Greedy entrepreneurs and businesses are taking advantage of the growing clean technologies. But, the media don't tell how it can affect the pockets of the taxpayers or how it will cost even more to install energy-efficient products within our home, business and the vehicle that we drive. It will also cause an effect on the taxpayers and cost for businesses become and to stay green.

Whether we Drill each Other or Unite

'Democrats, Republicans, Independents,
Conservatives & Liberals…This is not a Party…
This is the United States of America!'

Credits:

Copulos, Milton. Insight on the News, 9/30/2003, Vol. 19 Issue 21, p46-49, 3p; (AN10934937)

Meadows, William H. Insight on the News, 9/30/2003, Vol. 19 Issue 21, p47, 49, 2p; (AN10934939)

BLM, "Inventory of Onshore Federal Oil and Natural Gas Resources and Restrictions to Their Development." June 2008.

PIRGIM EDUCATION FUND: DIRTY DRILLING, www.pirgim.org

U.S. Fish and Wildlife Service: Opportunities Remain to Improve Oversight and Management of Oil and Gas Activities on National Wildlife Refuges: GAO-07-829R.

Source: GAO Reports; 7/30/2007, p1, 13p, 1 chart

Oil & Gas Drilling Industry Profile: Global; Mar2009, p1, 29p, 16 charts, 1 diagram, 7 graphs